DISCOVERING CAREERS FOR YOUR FUTURE

history

Ferguson Publishing Company
Chicago, Illinois

Carol Yehling
Editor

Beth Adler, Herman Adler Design Group
Cover design

Carol Yehling
Interior design

Bonnie Needham
Proofreader

Library of Congress Cataloging-in-Publication Data

Discovering careers for your future. History.
     p. cm.
  ISBN 0-89434-391-2
1.Vocational guidance—Juvenile literature. 2. History—Vocational guidance—Juvenile literature. [1.
History—Vocational guidance. 2.Vocational guidance.] I. Ferguson Publishing Company. II. Title: History

HF538.2.D573 2001
331.7'02—dc21

                                                 00-050296

Published and distributed by
Ferguson Publishing Company
200 West Jackson Boulevard, 7th Floor
Chicago, Illinois 60606
800-306-9941
www.fergpubco.com

Copyright © 2001 Ferguson Publishing Company
ISBN 0-89434-391-2

Printed in the United States of America
Y-4

Table of Contents

Introduction

You may not have decided yet what you want to be in the future. And you don't have to decide right away. You do know that right now you are interested in history. Do any of the statements below describe you? If so, you may want to begin thinking about what a career in history might mean for you.

___My favorite class in school is social studies or history.

___I enjoy reading about history in both nonfiction and fiction books.

___I often visit museum exhibits that show old objects and artifacts.

___I am interested in particular time periods in history (for example, the Civil War or ancient Egypt).

___I enjoy historical re-enactment events.

___I like to study dinosaurs.

___I am interested in societies and cultures and how they have changed throughout history.

___I know a lot about the history of my own town or community.

___I am working on tracing my family history.

___I think it's important to preserve old documents and artifacts.

___I enjoy shows and movies about historical periods and events.

___I like to do historical research in the library and on the Internet.

___I enjoy listening to my grandparents tell stories about their childhood.

___I am interested in the evolution and extinction of different species.

Discovering Careers for Your Future: History is a book about careers in history, from anthropologists to tour guides. People in history-related careers help us learn about our past. They collect information and uncover artifacts, fossils, documents, and anything that might lead to a better understanding of the natural world. They study such things as culture, language and writing, politics, and government as it has changed over time.

This book describes many possibilities for future careers in history. Read through it and see how the different careers are connected. For example, if you are interested in ancient history, you will want to read the chapters on Archeologists, Conservators and Conservation Technicians, Historians, Linguists, Museum Curators, and Paleontologists. If you are interested in museum work, you will want to read the chapters on Book Conservators, Conservators and Conservation Technicians, Costume Designers, Education Directors, Historians, Librarians, Museum Attendants and Teachers, Museum Curators, and Tour Guides. Go ahead and explore!

What do people in history careers do?

The first section of each chapter begins with a heading such as "What Archaeologists Do" or "What Historians Do." It tells what it's like to work at this job. It describes typical responsibilities and assignments. You will find out about working conditions. Which artists work in offices and libraries? Which ones work at archaeological digs in locations around the world? This section answers all these questions.

How do I pursue a career in history?

The section called "Education and Training" tells you what schooling you need for employment in each job—a high school diploma, training at a junior college, a college degree, or more. It also talks about on-the-job training that you could expect to receive after you're hired, and whether or not you must complete an apprenticeship program.

How much will I earn?

The "Earnings" section gives the average salary figures for the job described in the chapter. These figures give you a general idea of how much money people with this job can make. Keep in mind that many people really earn more or less than the amounts given here because actual salaries depend on many different things, such as the size of the company, the location of the company, and the amount of education, training, and experience you have. Generally, but not always, bigger companies located in major cities pay more than smaller ones in smaller cities and towns, and people with more education, training, and experience earn more. Also remember that these figures are current averages. They will probably be different by the time you are ready to enter the workforce.

What will the future be like for history careers?

The "Outlook" section discusses the employment outlook for the career: whether the total number of people employed in this career will increase or decrease in the coming years and whether jobs in this field will be easy or hard to find. These predictions are based on economic conditions, the size and makeup of the population, foreign competition, and new technology. Terms such as "faster than the average," "about as fast as the average," and "slower than the average," are terms used by the U.S. Department of Labor to describe job growth predicted by government data.

Keep in mind that these predictions are general statements. No one knows for sure what the future will be like. Also remember that the employment outlook is a general statement about an industry and does not necessarily apply to everyone. A determined and talented person may be able to find a job in an industry or career with the worst kind of outlook. And a person without ambition and the proper training will find it difficult to find a job in even a booming industry or career field.

Where can I find more information?

Each chapter includes a sidebar called "For More Info." It lists organizations that you can contact to find out more about the field and careers in the field. You will find names, addresses, phone numbers, and Web sites.

Extras

Every chapter has a few extras. There are photos that show artists in action. There are sidebars and notes on ways to explore the field, related jobs, fun facts, profiles of people in the field, or lists of Web sites and books that might be helpful. At the end of the book you will find a glossary and an index. The glossary gives brief definitions of words that relate to education, career training, or employment that you may be unfamiliar with. The index includes all the job titles mentioned in the book. It is followed by a list of general history Web sites.

It's not too soon to think about your future. We hope you discover several possible career choices. Happy hunting!

Anthropologists

Profile: Margaret Mead

Margaret Mead (1901-1978) was a pioneer in cultural anthropology. She made many studies of child-training methods. She studied the development of adolescents in the Samoan and Admiralty islands, which she described in the books *Coming of Age in Samoa* (1928) and *Growing Up in New Guinea* (1930). Later in her career she wrote about child development, personality formation, family life, feminism, cultural change, and national character (the customary attitudes of a people).

Margaret Mead received a Ph.D. degree from Columbia University in 1929. She joined the ethnology staff of the American Museum of Natural History in New York City in 1928 and was curator of ethnology, 1964-69. While on the museum's staff, she made a number of expeditions to the South Pacific islands and taught at Columbia and Fordham Universities.

What Anthropologists Do

Anthropologists study humans and how they have developed over hundreds of thousands of years. They are interested in the lifestyles and customs of groups of people in all parts of the world.

Cultural anthropologists study human behavior and culture. They look for things that will tell them about a people's religion, language, politics, or art. They interview people and observe them in their daily lives to learn about their customs, habits, and beliefs. Some anthropologists learn about the culture of a particular group of people by studying their weapons, tools, and pottery. Others study their language.

Physical anthropologists study the physical differences between people of past and present human societies. They compare human skeletal remains and the environments where they were found to trace the origin of different races. Many physical anthropologists also study other primates, such as chimpanzees and gorillas.

Urban anthropologists study the behavior and customs of people who live in cities. *Ethnologists* study tribal cultures that live in remote regions of the world.

Most anthropologists work for colleges, universities, or museums. They spend part of their time teaching anthropology, geography, or sociology. They may set up exhibits or catalog and store artifacts.

Some anthropologists travel a lot and are away from home for long periods of time. Sometimes they live in remote areas of the world and live in unfamiliar conditions. Anthropologists spend long hours taking notes, doing research, and writing about their work.

Education and Training

If you are interested in anthropology, concentrate on classes in history, English, writing, religion, and art.

Some beginning jobs in anthropology may be open to those who have bachelor's or master's degrees, but most anthropologists go on to earn a doctoral degree.

EXPLORING

• Participate in boys' or girls' clubs that offer exploration and camping trips.
• Learn about other cultures by attending local cultural festivals, music and dance performances, and religious ceremonies.
• Visit cultural centers and museums of natural history.
• Start thinking about The Earthwatch Institute's opportunities for high school students. Its Student Challenge Awards program gives selected students a chance to assist in the summer research of scientists. Recent projects have included an archaeological study with computer imaging at an ancestral Hopi village, and a study of rock art of the Malheur Marshlands in eastern Oregon. Contact the Earthwatch Institute, 3 Clock Tower Place, Suite 100, Box 75, Maynard, MA 01754; 800-776-0188; http://www.earthwatch.org.

There are many graduate schools that offer strong programs in anthropology and archaeology.

Earnings

According to the U.S. Department of Labor, college and university professors earned between $33,000 and $71,000, depending on the type of institution.

A 1998-99 survey by the American Asssociation of University Professors reported that the average salary for full-time professors was about $56,300.

For those who do not work at colleges and universities, the salaries vary widely. The National Association for the Practice of Anthropology estimates that anthropologists with bachelor's degrees start at about $16,000 a year. After five years of experience they can make $20,000 a year. Those with doctorates start at about $25,000 and work up to $30,000 with five years' experience. Midcareer anthropologists

READ ALL ABOUT IT

Here are some books that offer insight into the work of anthropologists. Look for more titles at your library or bookstore.

A Street Through Time by Annie Dillard (DK Publishing, 1998).

Ancient Civilizations: 3000 BC-AD 500 by the editors of Time-Life Books (Time Life, 1998).

The Bone Detectives: How Forensic Anthropologists Solve Crimes and Uncover Mysteries of the Dead by Donna M. Jackson (Little-Brown & Co., 1996).

Finding the Lost Cities: Archaeology and Ancient Civilizations by Rebecca Stefoff (Oxford University Press, 1997).

Wise Words of Paul Tiulana: An Inupait Alaskan's Life by Vivian Senungetuk and Paul Place for Winter Tiulana (Franklin Watts, Inc., 1999)

earn between $35,000 and
$75,000 a year.

Outlook

Most new jobs in the near
future will be nonteaching positions in consulting firms,
research companies, and government agencies. This is
because of growing interest in
environmental, historic, and
cultural preservation.

College and university teaching
has been the largest area of
employment for anthropologists
in the past. The demand for
professors is expected to
decline. Competition for teaching positions will be great even
for those with doctorates.

Employment for anthropologists
in both teaching and nonteaching positions should be about
as fast as average through
2008, according to the U.S.
Department of Labor.

FOR MORE INFO

*For more information about careers for
anthropologists, contact these organizations:*
**American Anthropological
Association**
4350 North Fairfax Drive, Suite 640
Arlington, VA 22203
703-528-1902
http://www.ameranthassn.org

Society for Applied Anthropology
PO Box 24083
Oklahoma City, OK 73124
405-843-5113
http://www.telepath.com/sfaa

RELATED JOBS

Archaeologists
College Professors
Geographers
Historians
Linguists
Museum Directors and Curators
Sociologists

Antique Dealers

What Antique Dealers Do

There are different categories of antiques, and different ways and reasons to collect them. Furniture, art, and jewelry are examples of antiques. Collectibles can be toys, tools, books, clothing, or automobiles. Many people collect postcards, theater programs, food labels, and baseball cards. Most *antique dealers* collect, buy, and sell a variety of previously owned household items. Some dealers specialize in items of a particular time period or style.

Antique shop owners, or proprietors, greet customers and answer any questions they may have. They clean the store, care for the antiques, and arrange store displays. They make records for new inventory and price it. Antique dealers also buy items. They inspect each piece and decide on a fair price to pay. They use *Kovel's Guide* and *Schroeder's Insider & Price Update* to look up guidelines and prices.

Antique dealers buy antiques at auctions, shows, and rummage sales. Many dealers take frequent buying trips, often to different parts of the country or overseas. Sometimes, dealers are invited to a person's home for a private estate sale.

Antique dealers can also be *appraisers*. They examine antiques to make sure they are authentic and not reproductions. They check for style details, signatures, and other markings. They evaluate an item's condition. Antique appraisers often become experts in very specific areas, such as Depression glass, 18th-century American furniture, Civil War memorabilia, or African-American art.

Education and Training

You can become an antique dealer with a high school diploma. Many successful antique dealers, however, have become specialists in their field through further education. Specialists often have advanced degrees in history, art history, fine art, or anthropology.

Some people begin their careers in antiques, learning on the job at antique shops. Others learn through their own personal collecting.

EXPLORING

• Visit antique stores and flea markets. Talk to salespeople and ask questions, such as: What makes an item valuable or not valuable? How much does an antique's condition affect its value?

• Watch public television's traveling antique show, *The Antiques Road Show.* People bring family treasures or rummage sale bargains for appraisal by antique industry experts. Visit their Web site at http://www.pbs.org/wgbh/pages/roadshow/. Click on "Appraisers" to learn more about the men and women who evaluate items on the show and how they became experts in antiques and collectibles.

• Check your library or bookstore for catalogs and manuals that describe styles and prices of antiques and collectibles.

WORDS TO LEARN

Americana describes almost any object—pottery, folk painting, furniture, and more. It not only refers to antiques made in the early era of this country, but it also refers to objects made overseas and sold to colonists.

Ephemera refers to anything short-lived, something that was not meant to last. A major area of ephemera is political campaign memorabilia, such as badges, buttons, and bumper stickers. Other examples of ephemera are 19th century Valentine's Day cards, 1930s and 1950s movie posters, inaugural ball tickets, and even promotional key chains given away by local retail stores.

The words **memorabilia** and **collectibles** are often used interchangeably. The dictionary defines memorabilia as "things that are remarkable and worthy of remembrance" or "things that stir recollection." This meaning suggests items that had a use before anyone thought to collect them. Examples are movie posters, sports programs, and animation cels. The dictionary defines a collectible as "suitable for being collected" or objects made just to be collected. Examples are Hummels or collector's edition plates meant to be displayed rather than used to serve food.

Earnings

Salaries depend on the type of merchandise sold, location of the store, and the current trends and tastes of the public. Some high-end stores dealing with expensive pieces and priceless works of art may make millions of dollars a year in profits. Most deal-

Early Antiques

The first interest in relics (other than those of religious significance) began in the Renaissance, when scholars became aware of the antiquities of ancient Greece and Rome. Monuments and buildings were admired. Statuary, coins, and manuscripts were collected and displayed in museums. Many ancient treasures were carried out of Italy, Greece, and Egypt before officials in those countries halted the removal.

It was not until after World War I that everyday objects of yesteryear began to be preserved and collected. As antiques became popular, the antiques business came into existence.

ers, however, are smaller and have less inventory. Also, some dealers work part-time, or rent showcase space from established antique shops. According to the Antiques & Collectibles Dealers Association, the average antique showcase dealer earns about $1,000 a month in profits.

Outlook

The antique industry, according to the ACDA, should experience average growth in future years. The Internet has helped some dealers increase their business. Most buyers, though, will continue to use more traditional ways of antique collecting. They want to see, touch, and examine the items they are interested in buying. The number of traditional antiques (items more than 100 years old) is limited, but the market should continue to grow.

FOR MORE INFO

To find out more about a career as an antique dealer, contact:
Antiques & Collectibles Dealers Association
PO Box 4389
Davidson, NC 28036
800-287-7127
http://www.acda.org

For information about appraisals or appraising, contact:
International Society of Appraisers
Riverview Plaza
16040 Christensen Road, Suite 102
Seattle, WA 98188-2965
206-241-0359
http://www.isa-appraisers.org

RELATED JOBS

Auctioneers
Conservators and Conservation Technicians
Historians
Museum Curators

Archaeologists

Visual Archaeology

Even artifacts of our own recent past can get easily lost in our fast-paced society. With that in mind, Frank Jump has climbed walls and crawled over fences to photograph the old painted advertisements fading from the walls of the buildings of New York City. These images, which he calls "visual archaeology," feature ads for Fletcher's Castoria, Baby Ruth candy bars, bobby pins, and Seely shoulder shapes. Some ads have faded partially to reveal other ads, creating multiple images. The photos have been exhibited at the New York Historical Society and are the subject of a photography book that Jump is creating.

What Archaeologists Do

Archaeologists study the physical evidence of people who lived in ancient times. They dig up, or excavate, the remains of ancient settlements, such as tools, clay pottery, clothing, weapons, and ornaments. They identify and study them to learn more about what life was like in the past.

Archaeologists often travel to places where ancient cultures once flourished. At the site, they carefully dig up any objects (artifacts) or remains of people, plants, and animals (realia) that remain from the culture. They try to clean, repair, and restore the artifacts as nearly as possible to their original condition. They study the realia to figure out what they looked like, what the people ate, how and where they lived, and how they survived.

Archaeologists must keep careful records. It is important to know exactly where each item was found and what its condition was. This can be very tedious work. Usually, when an archaeology team excavates an area, they brush the layer of dirt off one inch at a time with paint brushes, toothbrushes, and soft bristles. They save all the sand and dirt that they have brushed away. Another member of the team sifts this dirt with a fine screen to find any tiny bone fragments or chips of pottery.

In addition to research, archaeologists teach in colleges or universities or work in museums. Teachers give lectures, correct papers, and take students on field trips. Museum workers may also give lectures, as well as plan museum exhibits and work with the rest of the museum staff.

Education and Training

It takes years of study and special training to become an archaeologist. You should study as many modern and foreign languages as possible. Classes in English, writing, history, and social studies will be most helpful.

A bachelor's degree is the minimum requirement after high school. Most archaeologists have also earned a doctorate. If you want to be an archaeologist,

EXPLORING

• Scouting troops and other youth organizations often go exploring on camping trips.

• Visit nearby museums to see archaeological exhibits. Listen to lectures and talk to museum archaeologists to find out more about archaeology as a career.

• Read these and other archaeology books available at your library or bookstore:

Adventures in Archaeology by Tom McGowan (Twenty-First Century Books, 1997).

Finding Lost Cities by Rebecca Stefoff (Oxford University Press, 1998).

THE AMELIA EARHART PROJECT

The sudden disappearance of the world's most famous female pilot, Amelia Earhart, has haunted generations of archaeologists and historians. They believe she crash-landed near the island of Nikumaroro while trying to circle the globe in 1937. The International Group for Historic Aircraft Recovery (TIGHAR; pronounced "tiger") is planning a new expedition to the island. Over the years, TIGHAR researchers have recovered salvaged aircraft parts which appear to be consistent with the Lockheed Model 10E Electra flown by Earhart. They have also found a shoe of the same size and style worn by Earhart. The next expedition will involve excavation for the plane's engine and human remains. To learn more about The Earhart Project and the other projects sponsored by TIGHAR, visit their Web site at http://www.tighar.org.

The Oldest Musical Instrument

Researchers have uncovered what might be the oldest playable musical instrument, reports the scientific journal *Nature*. They found six complete bone flutes between 7,000 and 9,000 years old at the early Neolithic site of Jiahu in China.

The flutes are all made from the ulnae, or wing bones, of the red-crowned crane and have five, six, seven, or eight holes. You can hear an audio recording of the flute and read more about the discovery at http://www.bnl.gov/bnlweb/flutes.html.

Tests at the Music School of the Art Institute of China showed that the flute's seven holes produce a tone scale similar to the Western eight-note scale that begins "do, re, mi."

you should enjoy reading, studying, and writing, and have a strong interest in history.

Earnings

Archaeologists who work as professors earn average incomes of between $45,000 and $62,000 a year. Experienced archaeologists who do not work at colleges and universities earn annual salaries between $35,000 and $75,000 a year. According to the U.S. Department of Labor, social scientists earned about $38,900 in 1998.

Outlook

Most archaeologists work for colleges and universities, but in the future, there will be fewer teaching jobs available. This means that more archaeologists will look for work at research companies, government agencies, and large corporations. The fields of environmental protection and historical preservation are growing, providing more jobs for archaeologists.

FOR MORE INFO

At the AAA Web site, you can find valuable information about archaeology careers.

American Anthropological Association
4350 North Fairfax Drive, Suite 640
Arlington, VA 22203
703-528-1902
http://www.ameranthassn.org

Society for American Archaeology
900 2nd Street NE, Suite 12
Washington, DC 20002-3557
202-789-8200
http://www.saa.org

Archaeological Research Institute
181 North 200 West, Suite 5
Bountiful, UT 84025
http://www.ari-acrc.org

RELATED JOBS

Anthropologists
Archivists
Historians
Museum Curators
Sociologists

Archivists

What Archivists Do

Archivists work with manuscripts, battle plans, blueprints, photographs, maps, and legal documents. They decide which items should be saved and stored. They make records and prepare reference aids, such as indexes, descriptions, and bibliographies. These reference aids help researchers locate information in libraries and museums.

Archivists decide if written records should be preserved in their original form, on microfilm, or on computer files. Very old documents can be damaged by handling, so they must be copied in some way so that researchers can still use them to get information without destroying the originals. Archivists know how to handle and store paper and other materials so they remain undamaged. They also have to know how to repair any damage already done to old documents.

Archivists work for government agencies, corporations, universities, and museums.

When a customer needs information, archivists, much like librarians, must be able to quickly locate the correct documents using written or computerized records. They are extremely organized and pay close attention to details. Most archival work is quiet and solitary, but some archivists conduct tours and teach classes and workshops on history or document preservation.

Education and Training

Archivists usually need at least a master's degree in history or a related field. For some archivist jobs you need a second master's degree in archival studies or library science. Some positions require a doctorate (Ph.D.). After you earn a bachelor's degree, you may work as an assistant in a museum or library while you complete your education.

English, history, science, and mathematics are important for future archivists. If you have a special interest in a specific kind of archival work, such as medical history, you should take science courses such as anatomy, biology, and chemistry. Most employers do not require certification, but it is available from the Academy of Certified Archivists. To earn certification you must have practical experience

EXPLORING

• Visit a school or public library. Ask the librarian to explain how he or she decides which materials to keep in the collection and which to discard.
• Use archives for your own research. If you have a report due on Abraham Lincoln, for example, you could visit an archive or museum near your home that keeps some of Lincoln's personal papers and letters. A visit to the archives of a candy manufacturer could help you with a project on how a certain candy was invented and made. Be sure to contact the organization about your project before you make the trip.
• Keep your own family archive. Collect letters; birth, marriage, and death certificates; citizenship papers; special awards; photographs; and any other documents that provide facts about your family.

ARCHIVES GO DIGITAL

Archivists don't just sift through musty old papers. Many archivists are working to make archival collections available on computer, so people can have quick and easy access to records from around the world. Here is a small sample of archival collections that are available, in whole or in part, on the Web.

Library of Congress (http://lcweb.loc.gov/exhibits/)
Past exhibits include:
Sigmund Freud: Conflict and Culture
American Treasures of the Library of Congress
Religion and the Founding of the American Public
Frank Lloyd Wright: Designs for an American Landscape, 1922-32
Women Come to the Front: Journalists, Photographers, and
    Broadcasters During WWII
Declaring Independence: Drafting the Documents
Temple of Liberty: Building the Capitol for a New Nation
The African-American Mosaic: African-American Culture and History

Glenbow Archives (http://www.glenbow.org/archhtm/sampler.htm)
These archives in Calgary, Alberta, include:
Alberta Between the Wars, 1919-1939: The Photographs of William J.
    Oliver
Magic Lantern Slide Show
The "W" Files: Weird, Warped, and Wacky Offerings from Alberta's
    Archival Treasure Houses

Berkeley Digital Library (http://sunsite.berkeley.edu/collections/)
This site features the following online collections:
Aerial Photography Online
Anthropology Emeritus Lecture Series: UC Berkeley
Days of Cal: A Virtual Tour Through the History of the University of
    California, Berkeley
The Jack London Collection
Nineteenth-Century Literature
The Online Medieval and Classical Library: A Collection of Medieval
    and Classical Texts
Pictorial Highlights from UC Berkeley Archival Collections
Tebtunis Papyri Collection

in archival work, take certain courses, and pass an examination on the history, theory, and practice of archival science.

Earnings

Salaries for archivists vary depending on the employer and on the amount of education and experience you have. Archivists who work for the federal government or for famous museums usually make far more than those who work for smaller institutions or nonprofit organizations. Starting salaries for archivists with bachelor's degrees average about $22,600 annually at smaller institutions. The median annual salary for all archivists was $31,750 in 1998. The average annual salary for an experienced archivist working for the federal government was $57,500 in 1999.

Outlook

Job opportunities for archivists are expected to increase about as fast as the average through 2008. Competition for jobs is stiff. Those with specialized training, such as a master's degree or doctorate in history or in library science, will have better opportunities. Graduates who have degrees in archival work or records management will be in higher demand.

FOR MORE INFO

For more information about a career as an archivist, contact the following organizations:

Academy of Certified Archivists
Capitol Hill Management Services
48 Howard Street
Albany, NY 12207
518-463-8644
http://www.certifiedarchivists.org

American Institute for Conservation of Historic and Artistic Works
1717 K Street, NW, Suite 301
Washington, DC 20006
202-452-9545
http://palimpsest.stanford.edu/aic/

Society of American Archivists
527 South Wells, Fifth Floor
Chicago, IL 60607
312-922-0140
http://www.archivists.org/

Book Conservators

What Book Conservators Do

Book conservators treat the bindings and pages of books to help preserve them for the future. They repair books that have been damaged by misuse, accident, pests, or normal wear and tear.

Book conservators first examine books, judge how badly they are damaged, and decide how to fix them. They have to consider the book's history—a book bound by hand in Italy in 1600 will be repaired in a different way than a volume bound by machine in 1980.

When repairing a ripped sheet, book conservators use acid-free glue or a special acid-free book tape. High levels of acid in papers and materials make books wear away faster. All materials that a conservator uses are acid-free so they will last for many years.

If a book is falling out of its cover, conservators may need to glue the cover back on. If the cover is broken, the book will need a new cover. Conservators measure out the board and book cloth, cut materials to size, and glue the cloth onto the board. They size the bookblock (the book's pages), glue them, and set them in the cover. Conservators make sure that all materials are fitted in properly before the glue is dry.

For some rare books, a conservator may choose to make a box to house the book rather than repair a broken spine. Sometimes it's better to simply stop the damage instead of trying to repair it.

Sometimes bugs can cause damage by eating through paper, glue, and binding. Conservators make sure that all the bugs are dead, or take the books to a special place where chemical treatments will kill the mites before they fix the damage.

Education and Training

History, literature, art, foreign languages, chemistry, and mathematics classes will all help you build a strong background for book conservation.

Book conservators need to have thorough knowledge of bookbinding arts and papers. It is recommended that you earn

EXPLORING

• Learn all you can about how books are made. Study the history of books and binding. There are many "how to" bookbinding guides, such as *Basic Book-binding* by A. W. Lewis, *Hand Bookbinding: A Manual of Instruction* by Aldren A. Watson, or *ABC of Bookbinding* by Jane Greenfield.

• Try making a simple, hand-bound book to use as a journal or photo album.

• Contact the conservation or preservation department at your local library. They may offer tours of their facilities or workshops on the proper care of books.

• Community colleges, art museums, or community centers may have weekend or evening classes in bookbinding arts.

a bachelor's degree, even though it is not required. A degree in art, art history, or fine arts may help you get into a book conservation apprenticeship or internship program. After earning a bachelor's degree, you may wish to attend library school to earn a master's degree in library science.

Earnings

According to the U.S. Department of Labor, conservators and other museum workers had median annual earnings of $31,750

CONSERVE YOUR OWN BOOKS

- Keep books out of the sun. Ultraviolet rays can discolor materials and increase deterioration.

- Don't throw books around. Treat them with respect.

- Never bend pages to mark your place. Use a bookmark.

- Keep food and drinks away from books you are reading. Crumbs left in books can invite pests.

- Don't place books open face down on a surface. This can break the binding.

- Don't use books as coasters. Find something else to hold your drink!

- If you accidentally damage a library book, tell the librarian when you return it so it can be repaired before further damage occurs.

It's a Fact

- The ancestor of the modern book was the codex, invented in the second century. It was a collection of handwritten sheets fastened together at one edge. Before the codex, parchment was cut into rectangles and sewn together into long sheets that were made into rolls.
- The printing of books first developed in the Far East, where the Chiinese invented block printing. Each page was printed from a single carved wooden block.
- By the middle of the 13th century, paper began to replace parchment in bookmaking.
- Around 1450 printing with movable type was developed and by the end of the 15th century some 15 to 20 million copies of books had been printed.
- Books printed before 1501 are called *incunabula*, a Latin word meaning "cradle books."

in 1998. Bindery workers in 1998 earned an average of $9.95 an hour.

According to an independent survey, book conservators who are self-employed or work in a conservation center may earn anywhere from $20,000 to $70,000 per year.

Outlook

Employment of book conservators will probably grow about as fast as the average through 2008. Book conservators who are graduates of conservation programs should have good opportunities for employment.

Conservators work in libraries, museums, conservation organizations, large corporations, universities, or government agencies.

RELATED JOBS

Archivists
Bookbinders
Conservators
Librarians
Museum Curators

FOR MORE INFO

For more information about conservation topics, visit the Web site of CoOL (Conservation OnLine), a project of the Preservation Department of Stanford University Libraries.
Conservation OnLine (CoOL)
http://palimpsest.stanford.edu/

Guild of Book Workers
521 Fifth Avenue
New York, NY 10175
http://palimpsest.stanford.edu/byorg/gbw/

For information about preservation methods, services, and opportunities, contact:
Library of Congress
Preservation Directorate
Washington, DC 20540-4500
202-707-5213
http://lcweb.loc.gov/preserv/

For information on internship programs, contact:
Canadian Conservation Institute
1030 Innes Road
Ottawa, ON K1A 0M5 Canada
613-998-3721
http://www.pch.gc.ca/cci-icc

For information about how you can become a conservator, contact:
The American Institute for Conservation of Historic and Artistic Works
1717 K Street, NW, Suite 301
Washington, DC 20006
202-452-9545
http://aic.stanford.edu

Conservators and Conservation Technicians

Tips for Handling Artifacts and Art Work

1
Always wear gloves.

2
Support the base of the object. Do not lift or carry the object by its handles or appendages.

3
Large objects are weak— get help from other people.

4
Always set the object on a padded surface in its most stable position.

5
Do not rest paintings on the floor.

What Conservators and Conservation Technicians Do

Conservators and conservation technicians examine and judge the condition of artifacts and art objects. These objects may include natural objects, such as bones and fossils, or man-made objects, such as paintings, sculpture, metal, and paper. Conservation workers work in museums, historical societies, or state institutions. They usually specialize in a particular area of work, such as the preservation of books and paper, photographs, paintings, textiles, or wooden objects. Other conservators specialize in archaeological or ethnographical (human culture) materials.

The main job of conservators is to conserve or preserve items so that we can learn from them and continue to study them. They may study a Native American

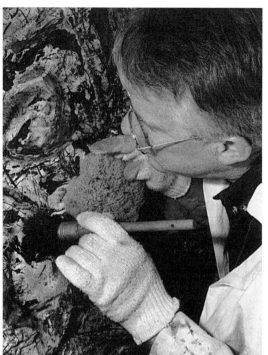

Mathew Hohmann

Conservators work at a painstakingly slow speed because the items they work on are usually priceless and irreplaceable.

ceremonial headdress to see its condition and stabilize its structure, for example. They decide on the best environment for the artifact to be stored and preserved. Areas that are too hot or too cold, or that are high in humidity can cause the item further damage. Conservators also document the condition of the object using written records and photography. A conservator's tools can include microscopes and cameras, including equipment for specialized processes such as infrared and ultra-violet photography, and X-ray processes.

Conservation technicians help conservators preserve and restore artifacts and art objects. They study descriptions and other information about the object. They may perform physical and chemical tests. If an object is metal, a technician may clean it by gently rubbing it with a cloth or by applying chemical solvents. Statues can sometimes be washed with soap solutions, while silver and some types of furniture can be polished. If an object is damaged, conservation technicians may reassemble the broken pieces using solder or glue. They may repaint an object if the original paint is missing or faded, using paint of the same color and chemical make-up as the original.

Education and Training

In the past, most conservation workers learned their craft as apprentices with experienced conservators. Today, most conservators have graduate training. First you must earn a bachelor's degree that includes classes in science (especially chemistry), the humanities (art, history, archaeology, and anthropology), and studio art. Then you go on to earn a graduate degree in conservation of art and historic works. Conservation technicians need at least some education beyond high school. You can begin to prepare for a career in historic conservation by concentrating on art, science, and social science classes.

Earnings

The average salary for a chief art museum conservator is $58,000. Senior conservators earn $40,000 to $61,000 a year. Associate conservators average $42,000 annually. Conservation technicians earn starting salaries of $18,000 to $25,000 per year.

The U.S. Department of Labor reports that in 1998 conservators, technicians, and other museum workers earned from $16,340 to $63,580 or more.

Outlook

The U.S. Department of Labor predicts the employment of conservators and conservation technicians will grow about as fast as average through 2008. Competition for these desirable positions, however, will be strong.

People will always be interested in cultural artifacts of all kinds, so there will continue to be a need for qualified conservation workers. Museums often

FOR MORE INFO

For information on conservation training, contact the following organizations:

The American Institute for Conservation of Historic and Artistic Works
1717 K Street, NW, Suite 301
Washington, DC 20006
202-452-9545
http://aic.stanford.edu/

The International Institute for Conservation of Historic and Artistic Works
6 Buckingham Street
London WC2N 6BA UK
01-44020-7839-5975

Arizona Studio of Art Conservation
1640 East Lind Road
Tucson, AZ 85719
520-323-6306

depend on government funds and grants, which can be uncertain. Private conservation companies and for-profit companies may offer more opportunities in the future for conservation workers than museums and nonprofit organizations.

Costume Designers

Starting at the Bottom

One of ancient man's first articles of clothing was protective covering for the feet. Animal hides were ideal for the purpose. In warm climates the typical footwear was the sandal, a sole with straps to hold it on. In colder climates, people wore shoes that wrapped around the foot and sometimes extended into boots. In ancient Greece and Rome the soles of soldiers' sandals were studded with hobnails, large-headed nails, for longer wear. Armies continued to use hobnail boots into modern times.

What Costume Designers Do

Costume designers create the costumes seen in the theater, on television, and in the movies. They also design costumes for figure skaters, ballroom dancers, and other performers. During the planning of a show, costume designers read the script. They meet with directors to decide what types of costumes each character should wear for each scene.

Stories that take place in the past, called period pieces, require costume designers to have a great deal of knowledge about what people wore during different historical time periods in different parts of the world. Designers do research at libraries, museums, and universities to study the garments, shoes, hats, belts, bags, and jewelry worn by men, women, and children. They look at the colors and types of fabric and how garments were made. Even for stories that take place in modern times or in the future, costume designers

Kranner Center for the Performing Arts

EXPLORING

• Join a school drama club or a community theater. Volunteer to work on costumes or props. School dance troupes or film classes also may offer opportunities to explore costume design.
• Learn to sew. Once you are comfortable sewing clothes from commercial patterns you can begin to try making some of your original designs.
• *The Costumer's Handbook* and *The Costume Designer's Handbook*, both by Rosemary Ingham and Elizabeth Covey, are good resources for beginning or experienced costume designers.
• Practice designing costumes on your own. Draw sketches in a sketchbook and copy designs you see on television, in films, or on the stage.

might use ideas that come from looking at the details of historical fashions.

Once the research is finished, designers begin to make sketches of their costume ideas. They try to design each outfit to look authentic, or true to the time period when the story occurs. Designers also pay attention to the social status of each character, the season and weather for each scene, and the costumes of other characters in each scene.

Costume designers meet with directors for design approval. They also meet with stage designers or art directors to be certain that the furniture and backdrops do not clash with the costumes. They meet with lighting designers to make sure that the lighting will not change the appearance of costume colors.

Costume designers decide whether to rent, purchase, or sew the costumes. They shop for clothing and accessories, fabrics, and sewing supplies. They also supervise assistants who do the sewing.

Education and Training

To become a costume designer, you need a high school education and a college degree in costume design, fashion design, or fiber art. You also need experience working in theater or film.

English and literature courses will help you read and understand scripts. History classes are helpful for researching historical costumes and time periods. Courses in sewing, art, designing, and draping are also necessary.

DON'T FORGET THE ACCESSORIES

Costumes include a lot more than clothing. Designers have to also consider accessories, such as these:

Belts and girdles, including sword belts, sashes, and suspenders
Neckwear, such as ruffs, collars, cravats, neckties, and tie clasps
Eyeglasses, including monocles, lorgnettes, and pince nez
Fans
Jewelry, including earrings, pins, necklaces, beads, bracelets, rings, and watches
Gloves
Purses and pouches
Shawls
Umbrellas and parasols
Walking sticks and canes

Earnings

Costume designers who work on Broadway or for dance companies in New York City

must be members of United
Scenic Artists union. A costume
designer for a Broadway musical with a minimum of 36
actors earns around $17,500.
For opera and dance companies, salary is usually by costume count. For feature films
and television, costume designers earn daily rates for an eight-
hour day or a weekly rate for an
unlimited number of hours.
Designers sometimes earn roy-
alties on their designs.

Most costume designers work
freelance and are paid per costume or show. Costume designers can charge between $90 to
$500 per costume, but some
costumes, such as those for figure skaters, can cost thousands
of dollars.

Outlook

Competition among costume
designers is stiff and will
remain so throughout the next
decade. There are many more
qualified costume designers
than there are jobs. Jobs will be
hard to find in small and non-

FOR MORE INFO

*This union represents costume designers in
film and television.*
Costume Designers Guild
13949 Ventura Boulevard, Suite 309
Sherman Oaks, CA 91423
818-905-1557

*This organization provides a list of schools
and scholarships and a journal. It has a college membership with opportunities to net-
work among other members who are professionals in the costume field.*
The Costume Society of America
55 Edgewater Drive
PO Box 73
Earleville, MD 21919-0073
410-275-2329
http://www.costumesocietyamerica.com

profit theaters, since they are
cutting their budgets or doing
smaller shows that require few
costumes. There may be more
opportunities in cable television, which is growing rapidly
and will continue to grow in
the next decade. New York
City and Hollywood are the
main centers for costume
designers.

Education Directors

Read All About It

From Knowledge to Narrative: Educators and the Changing Museum by Lisa C. Roberts (Smithsonian Institution, 1997).

Learning from Museums: Visitor Experiences and the Making of Meaning by John H. Falk and Lynn D. Dierking (Altamira Press, 2000).

Learning in the Museum by George E. Hein (Routledge, 1998).

What Education Directors Do

Education directors help museums and zoo visitors learn more about the exhibits they have come to see. Education directors plan and develop educational programs. These programs include tours, lectures, and classes that focus on the history or environment of a particular artifact or animal.

For example, a museum or zoo might focus on helping children understand more about the exhibits. In museums, children often are allowed to handle artifacts or play with objects. In zoos, children may be able to pet animals. Education directors develop special projects to help visitors learn more from this type of hands-on experience.

Education directors give teachers advice in how to lead workshops and classes. They help resource directors find materials, such as egg shells or skeletons, and instruments, such as microscopes, to use in their resource centers. They work with exhibit designers to create displays, perhaps showing the development of a moth into a butterfly, or display tools and artifacts used by ancient Egyptians. They also work with graphic designers to produce signs and illustrations that reveal more about an exhibit. Signs in a gorilla exhibit, for instance, may include a map of Africa to show where gorillas live.

Most education directors at museums work in art, history, or science, but other museums have a special interest, such as woodcarvings or circuses. These directors must have some training or experience in special fields, just as those at zoos must know about animals. Wherever they work, education directors must have a good knowledge of all the specimens in their collection.

Education and Training

Education directors usually begin in another position at a zoo or museum, perhaps as a teacher or resource coordinator. They are usually promoted into the position, or transfer between organizations to reach the director level. Education directors must have at least a bachelor's degree. Most positions require a

EXPLORING

• Most zoos and museums have student volunteers. Volunteers often help with tours, organize files or audio-visual materials, or assist a lecturer in a class.

• The American Association of Museums publishes an annual museum directory, a monthly newsletter, and a bimonthly magazine. It also published *Museum Careers: A Variety of Vocations, Resource Report 2, Part 1*, in 1988. This report is helpful for anyone considering a career in the museum field.

• *Introduction to Museum Work* by George Ellis Burcaw, published in 1983 by the American Association for State and Local History, discusses the educational programs at various museums.

master's degree, and many, including those at larger zoos and museums, require a doctorate.

Education directors often earn a bachelor's degree in liberal arts, history, or one of the sciences.

They go on to earn a master's degree in a specialized area of education.

Earnings

Salaries for education directors vary depending on the size,

A DAY IN THE LIFE OF AN EDUCATION DIRECTOR

7:30—Arrive at the museum. Check in at the security station and pick up identification badge.

7:45—Settle in office. Return phone calls and email.

9:00—Attend meeting with anthropology and history curators, exhibit designers, and museum taxidermist. Discuss plans for upcoming exhibit. Focus on exhibit design that will best represent objects and include thought-provoking interpretation for museum visitors.

10:30—Give tour of rainforest exhibit to second graders.

12:00—Give lunch lecture on Native American cradleboards to Civic Foundation members.

1:00—Lunch

1:30—Give tour of Egyptian exhibit to high school students.

2:45—Meet with education staff to develop ideas for instructional materials to use with the upcoming exhibit. Focus on materials for self-guided tours, families, and teachers.

4:15—Return phone calls and email messages. Open mail.

5:15—Prepare budget material for tomorrow's meeting with the director of finance and the museum director.

6:00—Stop at the security station and turn in badge.

type, and location of the institution, as well as the director's education and experience. The average beginning salary for education directors with bachelor's degrees and one year of experience is $23,000. Those with master's degrees may earn starting salaries of $33,000. The Association of Art Museum Directors reports that the average salaries for education directors are from $35,000 to $56,000 a year.

Outlook

The employment outlook for education directors is expected to increase more slowly than the average through 2008. Many museums and cultural institutions have cut their budgets and reduced the size of their education departments. Competition will be stiff for jobs in large cities and in well-known, popular institutions.

FOR MORE INFO

This organization provides information and training through publications, annual meetings, seminars, and workshops.
American Association for State and Local History
1717 Church Street
Nashville, TN 37203-2991
Tel: 615-320-3203
http://www.aaslh.org

For a directory of internships offered through public gardens, contact:
American Association of Botanical Gardens and Arboreta
351 Longwood Road
Kenneth Square, PA 19348
610-925-2500

For a directory of museums and other information, contact:
American Association of Museums
1575 Eye Street, NW, Suite 400
Washington, DC 20005
202-289-1818
http://www.aam-us.org

RELATED JOBS

Archivists
Librarians
Museum Attendants and Teachers
Museum Directors and Curators
Museum Technicians
Naturalists
Teachers and Professors

Foreign Service Officers

The Literary Connection

These famous writers have held diplomatic, consular, or senior posts with the U.S. State Department:

Washington Irving
"The Legend of
Sleepy Hollow"
Minister to Spain, 1842-46

Nathaniel Hawthorne
The Scarlet Letter
Consul at Liverpool, 1853-57

James Fenimore Cooper
The Last of the Mohicans
Consul at Lyon, 1826

William Dean Howells
The Rise of Silas Lapham
Consul at Venice, 1861-65

Archibald MacLeish
Conquistador
Assistant Secretary of State
for Public Affairs, 1944-45

What Foreign Service Officers Do

As members of the State Department, *foreign service officers* represent the United States throughout all parts of the world. They meet with government officials from other countries and report to the State Department on issues that could affect the United States. Officers also issue passports and give visas to persons visiting or moving to the United States. They help protect U.S. citizens in foreign countries, and help encourage U.S. trade overseas.

Specific job duties depend on an officer's area of expertise and the requirements of the overseas office. *Administrative officers,* for example, work in embassies and manage the day-to-day operations of the office. They plan budgets and hire local workers. They purchase and look after government property, sign contracts for office space and housing, and make arrangements for shipping and travel.

Consular officers provide medical, legal, and travel assistance to U.S. citizens traveling abroad in cases of accidents or emergencies. For example, they help those without money return home, help find lost relatives, and advise American prisoners in foreign jails. They also issue visas to foreign nationals who want to enter the United States.

Political officers pay attention to local developments and reactions to U.S. policy. They stay in close contact with foreign leaders and watch for changes in attitudes and leadership that may affect the United States. They report their observations to Washington, D.C., and may suggest changes in U.S. policy.

Foreign service officers also try to help promote U.S. trade overseas. They advise U.S. firms about business practices in foreign countries where those firms might want to open a new business.

Education and Training

English, math, social studies, and foreign language classes are important for future foreign service officers. You need a strong desire for public service and an interest in other cultures. You must be able to communicate with people whose

EXPLORING

• Join a foreign language club at your school.

• Research student exchange programs, if you're interested in spending several weeks in another country.

• The People to People Student Ambassador Program offers summer travel opportunities to students in grades six through 12. To learn about the expenses, destinations, and application process, visit their Web site at http://www.student ambassadors.org.

RELATED JOBS

Ambassadors
Congressional Aides
Federal and State Officials
Lobbyists
Political Scientists
Press Secretaries
Regional and Local Officials

PROFILE: JAMES PROSSER

James Prosser spent 36 years with the Foreign Service. He is now retired and visits academic and civic organizations to lecture about the history of the Foreign Service.

James's interest in foreign cultures started when he was very young. "Back in the 1930s," he says, "I built a crystal radio set which enabled me to listen to distant radio stations. That led me to discover shortwave listening, and soon I was listening to foreign countries."

As an officer, James worked in the telecommunications and computer fields as an operator, engineer, manager, and international negotiator. He speaks German, French, and Italian. His experiences included running a communications center and shortwave radio station in the Belgian Congo (now the Democratic Republic of the Congo) during the country's postcolonial independence. In 1967, France expelled North Atlantic Treaty Organization headquarters and James was placed in charge of moving the U.S. communications elements of NATO to Belgium, as well as designing the new communications facilities there. James also worked with Russians on the SALT (Strategic Arms Limitation Talks) delegations. James has served in Germany, Italy, Kenya, and other countries.

language, customs, and culture are different from your own.

Almost all officers have college degrees and many have master's degrees or doctorates in fields such as economics, political science, and mathematics. All foreign service officers are required to pass written and oral examinations. These examinations test applicants on their understanding of government institutions, geography, the history of the United States, foreign policy, and other subjects.

According to the American Foreign Service Association, foreign service officers need knowledge of proper English usage; U.S. society, culture, history, government, political systems, and the Constitution; world geography; and world political and social issues. In addition, all foreign service officers should know basic accounting, statistics and mathematics, and basic economic principles and trends.

Earnings

Earnings vary depending on experience, education, and foreign language skills. Starting salaries for new officers without a bachelor's degree are $29,911 a year. With a bachelor's or advanced degree and knowledge of a foreign language, officers can earn from $33,665 to $39,952 to start. Junior officers make up to $49,136 a year. Career officers make between $50,960 and $100,897, while senior foreign service officers earn $106,200 to $118,400.

Outlook

There are currently about 4,000 people working for the Foreign Service, in Washington, D.C., and overseas. The number of positions varies every year, and may be affected in the future by funding cutbacks in diplomacy and international affairs.

FOR MORE INFO

The U.S. Department of State has career information on its Web site, along with information about internships, the history of the Foreign Service, and current officers and embassies. Or write to request brochures.

Foreign Service
U.S. Department of State
2201 C Street, NW
Washington, DC 20520
202-647-4000
http://www.state.gov

For information about Foreign Service careers, contact:
American Foreign Service Association
2101 E Street, NW
Washington, DC 20037
800-704-AFSA
http://www.afsa.org

According to the American Foreign Service Association, foreign service officers of the future will need management skills and knowledge of issues, such as science and technology, including the global fight against AIDS, efforts to save the environment, anti-narcotics efforts, and trade.

Genealogists

Library Sources

There are important genealogical collections in these libraries:

The New England Genealogical Society Library, Boston

The Newberry Library, Chicago

The New York Public Library, New York City

The Library of the National Society, Daughters of the American Revolution, Washington, DC

The Church of Jesus Christ of Latter-day Saints has more than 200 genealogical libraries worldwide, all of which have access to the church's Genealogical Society's main library in Salt Lake City, the world's largest collection of genealogical records.

What Genealogists Do

Genealogists trace family histories. They examine historical and legal documents to find out when and where people were born, married, lived, and died. They research medical histories, adoption records, and military records. They work for lawyers, writers, filmmakers, or private clients. Anthropologists also use genealogy to record family relationships and ancestral lines of the cultures they study.

Today, genealogy is both a skilled profession and a hobby with many useful applications. Before a person can inherit title to land and property or be eligible for certain college scholarships, it is sometimes necessary to prove the lines of family descent. Membership in certain societies sometimes depends on a proper and proven family history. Most people, however, trace their genealogies because of curiosity about their ancestors or for the sake of information and enjoyment. In fact, genealogy has become the third most popular hobby in the United States, behind only coin and stamp collecting.

Genealogy is like historical detective work. The genealogist hunts for missing facts through research and deduction. Sometimes tracing a family history can be fairly straightforward. At other times, genealogists get stumped by incomplete records, dead ends, and conflicting information.

Genealogists often begin their research in the public library. They search for names and dates in telephone directories, census records, military service records, newspaper clippings, letter files, diaries, and other sources. County courthouses store a wealth of important data, including records of births, marriages, divorces, deaths, wills, tax records, and property deeds. A truly resourceful genealogist also will look for information in local newspaper records, school board records, clubs, churches and synagogues, immigration bureaus, and cemeteries.

Education and Training

If you are interested in becoming a genealogist, history, English, and geography classes are important. Knowledge of

EXPLORING

• Trace your own family history. Interview your grandparents, aunts and uncles, and other relatives to gather facts. Write down dates and places of birth, marriages, and deaths.

• Your community may have a local genealogical club, where members talk about their hobby, hold workshops, and share resources.

• Check your bookstore for books on tracing your family history. Many of them contain blank worksheets and forms.

RELATED JOBS

Anthropologists
Archaeologists
Archivists
Historians
Librarians
Title Searchers and Examiners

WHERE TO FIND FACTS

Home
Family Bible
Letters
Interviews
Photographs

County Records
Vital records
Marriage records
Wills, estates, deeds
Mortgages
Naturalization records

Town Records
City or county directories
Cemetery records
Newspaper files
Tax lists
Voter records
Public school records

Churches
Local parish records
Local church histories

State Records
Land grants
State census
Militia records
Tax lists

National Records
Censuses
Military records
Pension records
Passenger lists
Immigration records
Land records

Libraries
Indexes
Printed histories
Occupational histories
Obituary collections

foreign languages also can be valuable. You should develop research and library skills. Knowledge of computers is also important, because many libraries and archives now have computerized catalogs and research systems.

There are no formal requirements for becoming a genealogist. Many genealogists are self-taught or have learned the trade from established genealogists. But a college degree in genealogy, anthropology, history, English, or journalism can be an advantage.

Earnings

Because so many people in genealogy are hobbyists, and others work only part-time, it is difficult to estimate annual salaries. According to the Association of Professional Genealogists, self-employed genealogists charge between $15 and $100 an hour. Some experienced genealogists specialize in difficult research and earn higher fees.

Because the work is not steady or guaranteed, genealogists usually develop ways to supplement their income. They might write articles for magazines and journals or write a book on how to trace family history. Some genealogists teach courses in family history at community colleges, or public libraries.

Outlook

There will be few opportunities for genealogists in the future. Most genealogical work is done by people researching their own families. They consult genealogists about how to get started, and they may seek professional help when they run into problems or wish to uncover information in other parts of the country or the world.

Lawyers and people with legal claims sometimes employ genealogists to determine a person's right to a legacy, title, or family name. Societies whose members are required to prove a certain heritage, such as the

FOR MORE INFO

For information on careers and conferences in genealogical study, contact:
Association of Professional Genealogists
PO Box 40393
Denver, CO 80204
http://www.apgen.org

Board for Certification of Genealogists
PO Box 14291
Washington, DC 20044
http://www.bcgcertification.org/

For information on courses, careers, and resources in genealogy, contact:
National Genealogical Society
4527 17th Street North
Arlington, VA 22207
703-525-0050
http://www.ngsgenealogy.org

Daughters of the American Revolution, employ genealogists to verify the ancestral claims made by prospective members. Medical researchers are also beginning to trace family histories of people with genetic weaknesses and other hereditary illnesses in hopes of finding a cure.

Historians

What Historians Do

Historians study manuscripts, documents, artifacts, and other objects of earlier periods to learn about past civilizations. They write about their findings and teach others so that we can understand more about how the events and influences of the past have helped to shape our world today. Most historians are college professors. Others work in museums, libraries, historical societies, and for the government.

Historians usually specialize in a specific country, ethnic group, time period, or social movement. They may specialize in China, World War II, Indian tribes of the Great Plains, or the Civil Rights movement, for example. Some historians study historical trends and theories. For example, they might research how and why revolutions and wars happen, or how the development of religions affects political systems.

Historians spend most of their time in research and teaching. Research might involve visiting libraries, museums, and archives; interviewing people; or inspecting buildings and artifacts, such as tools, clothing, art, religious objects, and furniture. They analyze them and draw conclusions about the people who used them. Some historians work on preserving found objects. They often work in museums or cultural centers.

Historians must also be writers. They document their discoveries and ideas about what happened in the past. Because history is an ongoing process, it is important to keep accurate records.

Education and Training

If you are interested in history, concentrate on social studies, government, sociology, foreign language, and English classes. These classes will prepare you for college and help you develop writing and communication skills. For entry-level historian jobs, whether in teaching, museum, or historical society work, you need at least a master's degree in history. You need a doctorate to be a college or university professor. Many high schools still require only a bachelor's degree for

EXPLORING

• Do some research on a local historical figure or place. Visit your library and do Internet research. Visit your local office of city or county records to find information.

• Regularly visit museums, cultural centers, courthouses, or any other place that has historical objects and information. You may be able to find volunteer work conducting tours.

• If there is a particular time period that interests you, such as the Civil War or the American Revolution, you can easily find groups to join that will encourage your interests. Check for Internet sites, associations, re-enactment groups, and local organizations.

teaching, but some graduate study will give you better opportunities.

Earnings

Most historians work in colleges and universities. According to the U.S. Department of Labor, college and university professors start at about $42,000 a year in assistant professor positions. Associate professors earn about $50,000 a year. Full professors can make $70,000 a

WHERE DOES HISTORICAL INFORMATION COME FROM?

Relics and structures. Ancient ornaments, weapons, utensils, and bones provide historians with most of their information about early humans. From relics, or sometimes fragments of relics, they figure out how early humans lived, the state of their civilization, and what their world was like. Monuments, buildings, parts of buildings, and tombs can reveal a great deal about the religion, government, and culture of the people who built them.

Myths and legends. Myths and legends are not factual history, but they are often based on real events. They give clues to the customs and attitudes of the civilizations in which they started.

Written records. *Inscriptions* are fragments of early writing engraved on stone or clay tablets. Some describe important events. Others are records of legal agreements of business transactions. *Annals*, the earliest type of written historical record, were a listing of the year's events. Later, *chronicles* covered events over a period of years. They were continuous narratives of happenings arranged in order of occurrence. The true historical narrative was developed by the ancient Hebrews and Greeks. They not only described events, but also analyzed and interpreted them. Written records are not always reliable because they may contain misleading information, distortions, and even fiction. Sometimes there are conflicting accounts of the same events.

Other sources. Statistics and other materials can be analyzed with computers. Another valuable source is oral history, including tape-recorded interviews and reminiscences.

year. According to a 1998-99 survey done by the American Association of University Professors, full-time faculty earned about $56,300 a year. Full professors averaged $72,700 a year, and instructors about $33,400.

Outlook

Overall, the employment of historians will experience little growth in the next decade, although specialists in archival work may find more opportunities. Historians with a knowledge of computer software and databases will have an advantage. Competition will be stiff for full-time positions with colleges and universities. Some history majors will be able to work as trainees in administrative and management positions in government agencies, nonprofit foundations, and civic organizations.

FOR MORE INFO

To learn more about the careers of historians, contact these organizations:

American Historical Association
400 A Street, SE
Washington, DC 20003
202-544-2422
http://www.theaha.org

Organization of American Historians
112 North Bryan Street
Bloomington, IN 47408
812-855-7311
http://www.oah.org/

RELATED JOBS

Anthropologists
Archaeologists
Archivists
College Professors
Genealogists
Museum Directors and Curators
Secondary School Teachers
Writers

Librarians

What Librarians Do

Librarians are responsible for the books, magazines, newspapers, audiovisual materials, and other sources of information that are found in libraries. They purchase these materials, organize them, and lend them out. They also answer questions about the collections in the library and help people find the information they need.

There are many different types of libraries: college and university libraries, public libraries, school library media centers, and libraries containing rare or unique collections.

Public library work is probably the most familiar. Because there are many duties to perform, librarians often specialize in certain areas. *Library directors* are in charge of all the public libraries in a particular system. They supervise the *chief librarians* who run each of the branch libraries or the individual departments in large branch libraries. In large branch libraries, the chief librarians supervise those who head the various departments such as acquisitions, cataloging, and reference. *Acquisitions librarians* buy books and other materials for the library. *Catalog librarians* organize materials by subject matter. They give each item a classification number and prepare the cards or computer records that will help users find items. *Reference librarians* help readers find information in encyclopedias, almanacs, online computer databases, and other sources. *Children's librarians* help children select materials they would enjoy. They show children how to use the library, and organize special events such as story hours. *Bookmobile librarians* bring library services to rural and hard-to-reach places.

Not all librarians work in public libraries. Those who work in school library media centers also teach classes in library use. They help students with their assignments and select materials that teachers can use in the classroom. Some librarians work in special libraries, such as medical libraries. They purchase and organize materials of interest to a particular group of people—in this case, physicians, nurses, and medical assistants. Other special

EXPLORING

• Talk to your school or community librarian. He or she can give you a good idea of what goes on behind the scenes.

• Some schools may have library clubs you can join to learn about library work. Or consider starting your own library club.

• You might be able to work as an assistant in the school library or media center. You can check materials in and out at the circulation desk, shelve returned books, or type title, subject, and author information on cards or in computer records.

MILLIONS OF BOOKS

The 10 largest public libraries by number of volumes held are:

New York (NY) Public Library (The Research Libraries)	10,483,628
Queens Borough (NY) Public Library	9,510,814
Public Library of Cincinnati and Hamilton County (OH)	9,271,068
Chicago (IL) Public Library	9,222,449
Toronto (ON) Public Library	8,718,431
Free Library of Philadelphia (PA)	7,968,978
Boston (MA) Public Library	7,261,323
County of Los Angeles (CA) Public Library	6,883,210
Carnegie Library of Pittsburgh (PA)	6,632,303
Los Angeles (CA) Public Library	5,739,540

Source: Statistical Report 1999: Public Library Data Service (Chicago: ALA Public Library Association, 1999).

research libraries serve the science, business, engineering, and legal communities.

Education and Training

If you want to become a librarian, you should take classes in history, English, computers, and foreign languages.

After high school, you will need to earn a bachelor's degree, usually in the liberal arts. After college, you should attend a school accredited by the American Library Association and earn a master's in library science (M.L.S.) or master's in library and information science (M.L.I.S.). If you hope to advance to higher administrative levels in a library, you will need to earn a doctoral degree (Ph.D.) in library science or in a specialized subject area. Most states require school library media specialists, who work in grade school and high school libraries, to have a teacher's certificate in addition to a master's degree in library science.

Earnings

According to the U.S. Department of Labor, librarians earned about $38,500 a year in 1998. Salaries ranged from less than $22,900 to more than $67,800. Librarians working in elementary and secondary school earned about $38,900 and those in colleges and universities earned about $38,600. Librarians who worked in local government earned $32,600. In the federal government, the average salary for all librarians was about $56,400.

Outlook

The employment of trained librarians is expected to grow more slowly through 2008. Public libraries will be faced with higher costs and tighter budgets. They will rely more on volunteers, part-time employees, and support staff.

Employment opportunities will be best in nontraditional library

FOR MORE INFO

For more information about a career as a librarian, contact the following groups:

American Library Association
50 East Huron Street
Chicago, IL 60611
800-545-2433
http://www.ala.org/

American Society for Information Science
8720 Georgia Avenue, Suite 501
Silver Spring, MD 20910
301-495-0900
http://www.asis.org/

Special Libraries Association
1700 18th Street, NW
Washington, DC 20009-2514
202-234-4700
http://www.sla.org/

settings, such as information brokers, private companies, and consulting firms. The outlook is good for those skilled in developing computerized library systems and for those who are able to speak a foreign language.

Linguists

Linguistic Specialties

Anthropological linguistics is the study of language variation and use according to cultural patterns and beliefs.

Clinical linguistics uses linguistic theories to analyze disorders of spoken, written, or signed language.

Ethnolinguistics is the study of language in relation to ethnic types and behavior.

Geographical linguistics studies how languages and dialects are distributed in different regions.

Neurolinguistics is the study of how language is processed and stored by the brain.

Theolinguistics is the study of language used by theologians and religious scholars.

What Linguists Do

Linguists study the sounds, words, phrases, and sentences that make up languages. They also study how history and culture affect languages.

Linguists trace how languages and language families develop, where words come from, and how words get invented. They study languages that are spoken today as well as "dead" languages, such as Latin, which are no longer spoken. Some linguists focus on the way modern languages change and are influenced by cultural trends. Others, who specialize in the physical aspects of language, study how the lips, teeth, and tongue work to produce sounds. Their work can help people who have speaking problems or those who are trying to learn a language. Others study sign language and how gestures are used to communicate thoughts and ideas.

A linguist may specialize in one of many different areas. *Philologists* compare ancient and modern languages to learn about the origin and growth of language groups or families. For example, French, Spanish, and Italian are in the family called Romance languages. These languages evolved from their "parent" language, Latin. *Etymologists* study the history and development of words. *Special purpose linguists* study the languages for communicating in specific areas, such as science, medicine, religion, or computers.

Some linguists work for publishing companies or for the federal government. They may work as interpreters or translators. Most linguists work in colleges or universities, where they teach classes and work on research projects.

Linguistic research can cover a variety of subjects and can require travel, too. Linguists who study the language of ancient Egypt study writings found inside the pyramids. Those who study the languages of small, isolated groups of people often have to travel to the places where these people live.

EXPLORING

• Talk to people who speak other languages.

• Visit foreign countries if you have the chance. Do research before your trip to learn about the customs of the country you plan to visit and learn at least enough of the language to ask directions, shop in stores, or order food in a restaurant.

• Join a language club.

• Attend multicultural festivals and other events in your area.

RELATED JOBS

Anthropologists
College Professors
Computer Programmers
Interpreters and Translators
Sign Language and
Oral Interpreters
Speech-Language Pathologists
and Audiologists
Writers

ENDANGERED LANGUAGES

There are about 5,000 to 6,000 languages spoken in the world today, but that number is falling. Languages gradually disappear because cultures change. Sometimes people have to communicate with neighbors or invading societies and slowly lose their language and even their ethnic identity. Cultures that have been affected this way include the tribes of Papua, New Guinea; the native peoples of the Americas; national and tribal minorities of Africa, Asia, and Oceania; and European peoples, such as the Irish, the Frisians, the Provençal, and the Basques.

Many linguists are involved in preserving endangered languages. Some work in communities helping to develop teaching programs and encouraging people to use their language daily. They also might help document a dying language through videotape, audiotape, and written records of actual language use. They analyze the vocabulary and the grammar, and write dictionaries and reference grammars.

Education and Training

Linguists must be patient, curious, and exact, and have good reading, writing, and research skills. If you are interested in becoming a linguist, begin now to learn one or more foreign languages. You should concentrate on your classes in history, psychology, sociology, and other social sciences.

Employers of linguists usually require at least a bachelor's degree in linguistics, English, or a foreign language. Your course work may include: language and culture, the structure of English, linguistics and reading, bilingualism, and computer applications in linguistics. You need a doctoral degree to teach at a university.

University professors usually are involved in research projects in addition to teaching.

Earnings

A 1998 salary survey conducted by the *Chronicle of Higher Education* found that full professors at public universities received an average of $69,924 a year. Professors at private universities received $84,970 a year. Associate professors received an average of $50,186 annually at public universities and $56,517 at private ones. Assistant professors earned $42,335 at public universities and $47,387 at private schools.

Outlook

There will be more trained linguists than jobs available in the coming decade. Linguists may find jobs in new areas, such as developing new computer languages. Also, as more companies conduct business internationally, they will need linguists to interpret and translate during negotiations. Literacy programs both in the United States and in other countries may also offer opportunities for linguistic work.

FOR MORE INFO

For information about linguistic programs at colleges and universities, contact:
Linguistic Society of America
1325 18th Street, NW, Suite 211
Washington, DC 20036
202-835-1717
http://www.lsadc.org

For information about employment and membership, contact:
Modern Language Association of America
26 Broadway, 3rd Floor
New York, NY 10004-1789
646-576-5000
http://www.mla.org

Kids Communicate

In 1880, immigrants were brought to Hawaii to work in the sugar industry. Their children—Spanish, Japanese, and Korean—played together and formed their own language to communicate. The parents learned the new words and phrases from their children, and Hawaiian Creole evolved into a sophisticated language by 1910.

Museum Attendants and Teachers

The term *museum* is from the ancient Greek word meaning "a place sacred to the Muses." The Muses were nine Roman goddesses who presided over literature, the arts, and the sciences.

The word museum was used for an institution for literary and scientific study founded in Alexandria, Egypt, in the third century BC. The term came into use again in the 15th century. In Italy scholars kept their collections of historical material in rooms they called museums. Renaissance nobles adorned their palaces with art, sculpture, and collections of curiosities. Later many private collections passed to public ownership and were put on display.

The British Museum, the first museum operated as a national institution, was founded in 1753.

What Museum Attendants and Teachers Do

Museum attendants protect museum collections and help museum visitors. They are sometimes called museum guards because they protect the exhibits from harm. They inform visitors of museum rules and regulations. Sometimes this means preventing patrons from touching a display, or warning children not to run through the halls. If an exhibit is popular and draws a large crowd, museum attendants keep everyone orderly.

In some museums, the attendants may have to check the thermostats and climate controls. A priceless document or work of art can be as easily destroyed by humid conditions as it can by careless hands. Attendants report any damage or needed repairs to the museum curator.

Museum attendants are the main source of information for museum visitors. They know about the exhibits as well as the

Children's Nature Museum is a special feature of the Academy of Natural Sciences of Philadelphia. Here a museum teacher teaches some youngsters about reptiles.

museum itself. Attendants answer questions from people of all ages and cultural backgrounds.

Most museums hold lectures, classes, workshops, and tours to teach the public about what is in the museum and why it is there. *Museum teachers* conduct all the educational programs. For special exhibits, the museum teacher works with the museum curator to develop written materials, such as pamphlets to be handed out at the display, books to be sold in the gift shop, or study guides for students. Museum teachers arrange and

EXPLORING

• Participate in museum programs, such as field trips, photography clubs, study groups, and behind-the-scenes tours.

• Talk to your local museum officials about any volunteer opportunities available.

schedule classes for children and adults. They have strong communication skills and creativity to make these programs interesting to people of all ages and cultural backgrounds.

Education and Training

A high school diploma is required for museum atten-dants. Employers are more likely to hire those with college education or experience working in a museum. Attendants usually are trained on the job where they quickly learn about all the objects in the museum's permanent collection. They get additional training to learn about any special temporary exhibits.

WEIRD AND WACKY MUSEUMS

When you think of museums, you might first think of natural history, science, or art museums. But people have collected some strange items and opened museums to display them.

The Burlingame Museum of Pez, San Francisco, California, has hundreds of dispensers from the 1950s to the present.
http:/www.burlingamepezmuseum.com

The Banana Museum, Auburn, Washington, has nearly 4,000 banana-related items. http://www.geocities.com/napavalley/1799/

The Toaster Museum, Charlottesville, Virginia, not only has pop-up toasters, but toaster art, toys, and accessories. http://www.toaster.org

More weird museums are described in *Offbeat Museums: The Collections and Curators of America's Most Unusual Museums* by Saul Rubin (Santa Monica Press, 1997).

Museum teachers need a college-level education with classes in both education and a specialty. For example, teachers in art museums have studied art history and education. Many colleges offer courses in museum studies (museology), which are valuable in the competitive field of museum work.

Earnings

Large museums in big cities pay more than smaller regional museums. Salaries for museum attendants range from $9,000 to $29,000 a year. The average salary for an educational assistant ranges from $22,000 to $32,000. An associate educator earns $36,000 on average. Museum teachers with experience who work in large museums earn about $44,000 a year.

Outlook

The education services provided by museum attendants and educators are an important part of a museum's operations. That means museums will expect greater professionalism, more

FOR MORE INFO

For information on careers, education and training, and internships, contact:
American Association of Museums
1575 Eye Street, NW, Suite 400
Washington, DC 20005
202-289-1818
http://www.aam-us.org

This association for anyone interested in art education has student memberships.
National Art Education Association
1916 Association Drive
Reston, VA 20191
703-860-8000
http://www.naea-reston.org

education, and specialization in the future for high-level positions. Since budgets are small and often unstable, museums will depend on volunteer attendants and teachers. Competition for paid jobs will be stiff.

Museum Curators

Read All About It

America's Science Museums by Victor J. Danilov (Greenwood Publishing Group, 1991).

America's Smithsonian: Celebrating 150 Years by I. Michael Heyman (Smithsonian Institution Press, 1996).

Children's Museums: An American Guidebook by Joann Norris (McFarland & Company, 1998).

Introduction to Museum Work by George Ellis Burcaw (Altamira Press, 1994).

Museum Basics by Timothy Ambrose and Crispin Paine (Routledge, 1993).

What Museum Curators Do

Museum curators take care of all the objects in a museum's collection, including items in storage, as well as those on display. They also search for new items for the museum to purchase, trade, or receive as donations. Curators make sure that the items are properly cataloged— numbered, described, and stored away— so that they can be easily found when needed. Keeping records is an important part of the curator's job.

Museum curators make sure that collections are in good condition. This includes repairing and restoring damaged pieces, as well as making sure that objects stay in good condition. Delicate items must be kept out of direct sunlight or stored where the humidity is not too high. Some curators are specialists in one area, such as paintings, textiles, or ceramics.

Museum curators decide which items are displayed and sometimes help with ideas for exhibit designs. They work with museum teachers to research and gather information for museum publications, such as booklets, maps, charts, and the labels that describe the exhibits.

Curators are sometimes involved in fund-raising. They organize events and solicit donations to make money to purchase new items for the museum. Curators today must also be up-to-date with the latest computer technology for cataloging large collections and making information available to researchers over the Internet.

EXPLORING

• Participate in clubs that involve fund-raising activities. Becoming the president of one of these clubs can give you experience in supervising and leadership.

• Sign up for any programs your local museum may offer, such as field trips or tours.

• Ask if there are any volunteer oportunities for students at your local museums.

Education and Training

English, business, and foreign language classes are all good classes to take in preparation for a career as a museum curator. You must have a college degree to become a museum curator. Most curators have doctorates in their area of specialty, such as art history, Renaissance history, or Latin American culture. Some assistant curators have master's degrees. Many colleges and universities offer courses in museum studies (museology). The best and most valued training is museum experience as a volunteer or another lower-level museum job.

Earnings

According to the U.S. Department of Labor, median annual earnings of archivists, curators, museum technicians, and conservators in 1998 were $31,750. Salaries ranged from less than $16,300 to more than $63,600. The Association of Art Museum Directors reports that entry-level curators, often called curatorial assistants or curatorial interns, earn about $24,000 a year. Assistant curator salaries average from $26,000 to $37,000 a year. Associate curators and curators of exhibitions average $34,000 to $53,000 a year. Chief curator salaries average $57,000, but may be considerably higher or lower depending on the demands of the job and the museum's overall budget. Curators who direct an ongoing program of conservation and acquisitions in large, national or international urban

PRICING THE PRICELESS

Placing value on items in museum collections is often a difficult task. Generally the older, rarer, and better preserved items are the most valuable. Here are some questions curators ask to determine pricing for insurance purposes.

- How many of these items exist in this museum's collection?

- How many of these items exist in museum collections in the United States?

- How many of these items exist in museum collections in the world?

- Has this item been used, or is it brand new?

- What is this item made of?

- Does this item have a notable history?

- What condition is this item in?

- Who made this item?

- Is this item made anymore?

- Where is this item from?

museums earn the highest salaries—as much as $152,000 a year.

Outlook

There are few openings for museum directors and curators and competition for them is stiff. New graduates may have to start as interns, volunteers, assistants, or research associates before they find full-time curator or director positions. The employment outlook for museum directors and curators is expected to increase about as fast as the average through 2008, according to the U.S. Department of Labor. The best opportunities are in art and history museums.

Curators of the future must be able to develop public programs that make money for the museum, since museums are subject to the availability of grants and other charitable funding. They must be able to start joint research programs with other institutions (museums or universities).

FOR MORE INFO

For information on careers, education and training, and internships, contact:
American Association of Museums
1575 Eye Street, NW, Suite 400
Washington, DC 20005
202-289-1818
http://www.aam-us.org

This organization represents directors of the major art museums in North America. It sells a publication on professional practices, a salary survey, and a sample employment contract.
Association of Art Museum Directors
41 East 65th Street
New York, NY 10021
212-249-4423
http://www.aamd.org

RELATED JOBS

Anthropologists
Archaeologists
Archivists
Biologists
Conservators
Ecologists
Education Directors
Historians
Museum Attendants and Teachers
Teachers

Paleontologists

Man or Medicine?

In the 19th century, some Chinese pharmacists made regular trips to a limestone hill near Beijing to dig for fossils. Their purpose was not research, but to collect the fossils for grinding into medicine. The bones they collected were later recognized as "near-human," dating from about a half-million years before. In 1929, part of a skull was discovered in the same location, as well as a new species, Peking Man, that preceded *Homo sapiens* in the evolutionary chain.

What Paleontologists Do

Paleontologists examine rocks and fossils. Fossils are the remains or traces of prehistoric plants and animals that were preserved in the rocks of the earth.

Paleontologists study rock formations to learn more about the history of life on earth, the placement of land and water, and the location of important substances, such as oil, gas, and coal. Rocks give clues about ancient environments and climates.

Fossils help paleontologists figure out the age of rocks on the earth. Once the age of the fossil is determined, then scientists can estimate the age of the surrounding rock. Paleontologists also study fossils, to figure out the age of a particular type of plant or animal. They determine when it lived, and compare it to similar plants and animals from various time periods. This helps them trace the animal or plant's evolution to see how it has changed or adapted from one time period to the next.

Paleontologists spend a lot of time in laboratories. They also travel throughout the world to work in the field—sometimes for months at a time—collecting specimens to examine. Field work is sometimes painstaking. It takes patience and dedication to gather and interpret detailed information about the earth. Paleontologists use dynamite and jackhammers, masonry hammers, chisels, putty knives, trowels, sifters, and soft-bristled paint brushes. They always carry a notebook and pen or pencil to make detailed notes.

Education and Training

Paleontology is a subspecialty in the field of geology. Paleontologists usually study geology in college, although a few major in such fields as botany or zoology. After college, they go on to study paleontology in graduate school.

Most paleontologists earn a doctoral degree (Ph.D.). Those with master's degrees may be able to find work as technicians, either as preparators, collections managers, or lab supervisors. Those who wish to do research, exploration, college-

EXPLORING

• Check with a local museum about field trips open to the public. The museum may also be able to direct you to local rock- or fossil-collecting clubs.

• Contact your state geological society for information about fossils in your area, and fossil-hunting outings.

• The Midwest and Great Plains states are especially rich in fossil beds. This is because an inland sea once covered these areas. Sediments from this sea protected the skeletons of creatures and kept them from being moved about.

• Professional geology societies publish brochures on fossil hunting and the kinds of fossils available in different areas.

level teaching, or museum work will need a doctorate.

Paleontologists usually work on teams with other scientists, so it is important to learn communication skills. You will need computer skills to handle the large amounts of data.

Earnings

The American Geological Institute estimates that experienced paleontologists with

FOSSIL HUNTING TIPS

Where do you find fossils? Quarries, roadcuts, and cliffs are good places to find fossils. Remember safety first, and you may need special permission to explore some areas.

Many state geological offices sell maps and books on the state's geology, including paleontology. Check with the U.S. Geological Survey or your public library for publications and reports on the paleontology of your area. Also try the bookstore of a natural history museum.

There may be an amateur paleontology organization in your area. It may publish information or sponsor fossil-hunting expeditions.

There are rules and laws for fossil-hunting in your area. It is up to you to find out what they are. Usually you need permission from the owner to collect on private land. You need a permit to collect in national parks and land managed by the Bureau of Land Management. Remember not to deface sites, litter, or put yourself or others in any danger.

RELATED JOBS

Archaeologists
Ecologists
Geologists
Museum Curators
Naturalists

bachelor's degrees in the geological sciences can make about $40,000 a year. Those with doctorates can earn as much as $77,000 a year.

According to the American Association of University Professors 1998 salary survey, professors who teach in doctoral programs made an average of $61,800 a year, compared to $45,200 for those who teach at four-year institutions.

Outlook

There are few job openings for paleontologists, so the competition is stiff. More paleontologists graduate every year than there are positions open for them. There are also fewer educational opportunities, as schools close geology departments in order to cut costs. To increase opportunities for employment, paleontologists will have to train in other areas, such as zoology or botany.

FOR MORE INFO

For a brochure on careers in the geological sciences, as well as information about scholarships and internships, contact:
American Geological Institute
4220 King Street
Alexandria, VA 22302
703-379-2480
http://www.agiweb.org

Geological Society of America
3300 Penrose Place
PO Box 9140
Boulder, CO 80301-9140
303-447-2020
http://www.geosociety.org

For career information, contact:
Paleontological Research Institution
1259 Trumansburg Road
Ithaca, NY 14850
607-273-6623
http://www.englib.cornell.edu/pri/pri1.html

For general information on paleontology, contact:
Paleontological Society, Inc.
Box 28200-16
Lakewood, CO 80228
http://www.uic.edu/orgs/paleo/homepage.html

The Society of Vertebrate Paleontology
PO Box 809183
Chicago, IL 60680
http://www.museum.state.il.us/svp/

Political Scientists

Read All About It

These books can give you an idea of the variety of interests within political study:

Acting in Concert: Music, Community, and Political Action by **Mark Mattern (Rutgers University Press, 1998).** This book examines the political aspects and purposes of popular music.

Political Science Fiction edited by **Donald M. Hassler and Clyde Wilcox (University of South Carolina Press, 1997).** This collection of essays examines the close relationship between politics and science fiction.

Twenty Years of Censored News by **Carl Jensen (Seven Stories Press, 1997).** This book discusses the most overlooked news stories of the last 20 years. It questions the political responsibilities of the news media.

What Political Scientists Do

Political scientists study government and politics. They teach, write, and do research to solve problems and create new theories. They act as advisors to politicians, political groups, businesses, and industries.

Political scientists often specialize in one aspect of government or politics. For instance, they may concentrate on American government or on international relations. Or they may specialize in law, political parties, or the history of political ideas. Fields of political science also include citizenship, comparative government (forms in various countries), public administration, public opinion, and constitutional law.

Political scientists work with historians, economists, policy analysts, and other professionals to compile information. They use the Internet and libraries to access government documents. They also use information from professional journals, encyclopedias, law books, and personal letters. Once political scientists gather the information, they analyze it, then write about their theories. These theories help government leaders make decisions and help businesses negotiate with each other.

Most political scientists work as college and university instructors. Their responsibilities are divided between teaching and research. Teachers lead seminars, assign papers, and advise students majoring in political science.

Political scientists also work for government and public agencies. They may help form public policy, advise on international relations, or hold other administrative positions.

Education and Training

Courses in government, history, English, and math will prepare you for a career in political science.

Most political scientists hold doctoral degrees. An undergraduate program includes courses in English, economics, statistics, American politics, international

EXPLORING

• There are numerous books in your local or school library that detail careers in political science.

• Write to college political science departments for information about their programs. You can learn a lot about the work of a political scientist by looking at college course lists and faculty biographies.

• When you turn 16, you can contact the office of your state's senator or representative in the U.S. Congress about applying to work as a page. Page positions, although hard to get, allow students to serve members of Congress, running messages across Capitol Hill in Washington, D.C. This experience would teach you about the workings of government.

THE LIBRARY OF CONGRESS: A Research Tool

The government has long been involved in expanding and developing the World Wide Web. These efforts have included making a lot of government information available on the Internet to political scientists and the general population. The Library of Congress homepage (http://www.loc.gov) is a particularly useful site to researchers. The site includes:

- Access to catalogs of the Library of Congress and other libraries
- Various databases
- Search tools for blind and physically handicapped persons
- Access to copyright records
- Documents, photographs, movies, and sound recordings that represent American history
- Online versions of exhibitions that have been featured at the library in Washington, D.C., such as Votes for Women 1848-1921and the Spanish-American War in Motion Pictures

politics, and political theory. Graduate study includes courses in public opinion, political parties, and foreign policy design. Students in graduate school also assist professors with research, attend conferences, and teach undergraduate courses.

Earnings

The U.S. Department of Labor reports that median annual earnings for social scientists in 1998

FYI

Nicolo Machiavelli (1469-1527) is sometimes called the first modern political scientist. In *The Prince,* he describes how rulers act ruthlessly in statecraft.

Other early political scientists include these:
French writer **Jean Bodin** (1530-96) believed in the concept of state sovereignty under an absolute monarchy subject only to God and natural law.
English philosopher **Thomas Hobbes** (1588–1679) upheld absolute sovereignty and believed that humans could escape the lawless "state of nature" only by a social contract that grants a sovereign ruler absolute power to preserve peace.
English philosopher **John Locke** (1632-1704) defended the right to revolt against an unjust ruler.

were $38,990. Salaries ranged from less than $21,530 to more than $80,640.

Full professors at public universities earn an average of $69,924 a year. Professors at private universities receive $84,970 a year. Associate professors earn around $53,000 and assistant professors earn $45,000 a year.

Outlook

Overall employment of social scientists is expected to grow about as fast as the average through 2008, according to the U.S. Department of Labor. One of the main employers of political scientists is universities. There will be heavy competition for the few graduate assistantships and new faculty positions available. Also, there's not a great deal of movement within the field because professors generally stay in their positions until retirement.

FOR MORE INFO

For more information, contact:
American Political Science Association
1527 New Hampshire Avenue, NW
Washington, DC 20036
202-483-2512
http://www.apsanet.org

Canadian Political Science Association
260 Dalhousie Street, Suite 204
Ottawa, ON K1N 7E4 Canada

RELATED JOBS

Ambassadors
Congressional Aides
Federal and State Officials
Foreign Service Officers
Lobbyists
Press Secretaries
Regional and Local Officials

Research Assistants

What Research Assistants Do

Research assistants help find facts, information, and statistics. They work for scientists, editors and writers, publishers, film makers, attorneys, and advertising executives, among others. Today, almost every field imaginable hires research assistants to help get jobs done more thoroughly and quickly.

After they receive an assignment, research assistants decide how to find information. They may spend hours, days, or even weeks of research in archives, libraries, laboratories, museums, on the Internet, or by talking to experts. Research assistants write up notes or a report of the information.

Research assistants who work for writers or editors help find statistics or other information for a specific article or book. Some research assistants called *fact checkers* make sure that facts, such as dates, ages, and numbers are correct before they are published.

Research assistants who work in radio, film, and television might help to find and verify historical information or locate experts to be interviewed.

Research assistants who work in the sciences, engineering, or medicine help scientists find background information for their experiments.

University professors hire research assistants, often graduate students, to help them in their research. For example, a history professor working on a paper about the Italian military might send a research assistant to the library to uncover everything possible about the Italian military presence in Greece during World War II.

Advertising agencies and marketing departments hire research assistants to help them decide how and when a product should be sold.

Law firms hire research assistants to find out facts about past cases and laws.

EXPLORING

• **School assignments provide opportunities to see if you enjoy research. Experiment with different types of research using newspapers, magazines, library catalogs, computers, the Internet, and official records and documents.**

• **Work as a reporter for your school newspaper, or volunteer to write feature articles for your yearbook. You can research the history of your school, the history of its sports programs, or famous alumni.**

• **Ask a librarian or bookstore clerk to help you find books on how to do research. A resource librarian would be glad to talk to you about the many research tools you can find there.**

Politicians hire research assistants to help find out how a campaign is succeeding or failing, to find statistics on outcomes of past elections, and to determine the issues that are especially important to the constituents.

Education and Training

History, English, mathematics, and foreign language classes are good preparation for this career. Pay special attention to your writing and research skills. Since electronic research is becoming more important, you should take classes in computers. If you are interested in science and engineering research, you should take all the laboratory courses you can.

Education requirements vary, depending upon the field in

WHAT IS AN INFORMATION BROKER?

Information brokers are basically the same as researchers. They perform online searching and library research for business, industry, government, academic, and scientific communities. They are also called *information consultants, independent researchers, freelance librarians,* or *informationists.*

Information brokers usually earn hourly fees, from $20 to $40, for finding information. The main types of information services they offer are:

• Online research (Internet and commercial databases)

• Manual research (libraries)

• Document delivery (finding actual documents)

• Public records research (both online and manual)

• Telephone research

which you work as a research assistant. Most employers require an undergraduate degree. Some fields, especially the sciences, engineering, and law may require you to have an advanced degree or other special training.

Earnings

Salaries for research assistants vary, depending upon the field of research and the size and resources of the employer. Those who earn the largest salaries often work in the sciences for large companies or laboratories such as in the pharmaceutical industry.

Research assistants who work part-time for a professor while earning a graduate degree generally earn $12,500 a year. Full-time research assistants earn from about $22,800 to $52,000 a year.

Outlook

The job outlook varies depending upon the field. A researcher with good background in many

FOR MORE INFO

Association of Independent Information Professionals
7044 South 13th Street
Oak Creek, WI 53514-1429
414-768-8001
http://www.aiip.org

For information on research assistant positions with the U.S. Census Bureau, contact:
U.S. Census Bureau
Washington, DC 20005
301-457-4100
http://www.census.gov/

The Library of Congress Services for Researchers
http://lcweb.loc.gov/rr/

fields will be in higher demand, as will a researcher with specialized knowledge and research techniques specific to a field. The best opportunities will be for highly skilled research assistants who are trained in the sciences.

Sociologists

Sociology Specialties

Here are some of the areas sociologists can specialize in:

Families

Adolescents or children

The urban community

Education

Health and medicine

Aging and the life course

Work and occupations

The environment, science, and technology

Economics, social inequality, and social class

Race relations, ethnicity, and minorities

Sex and gender

Sports

Culture and the arts

Politics, the military, peace, and war

Crime, delinquency, law, and justice

Social change and social movements

What Sociologists Do

Sociologists study the various groups that people form. They study families, tribes, communities, and other social and political groups to understand how they develop and operate. Sociologists observe these groups and record what they find. Besides observing groups themselves, sociologists may use population counts, historical documents, and tests. To gather information, sociologists interview people, or distribute questionnaires. They conduct surveys and set up experiments that place people in certain kinds of interaction. They may study how people of different races relate, how people of opposite genders communicate, and how communities are affected by different religious practices and belief systems. Lawmakers, educators, and others then use the information to help solve social problems.

A sociologist can specialize in one field. *Criminologists* study causes of crime and ways to prevent it. *Urban sociologists* study cities and the ways people live within them. *Industrial sociologists* specialize in the relationships between employees in companies. *Clinical sociologists* study groups that do not work well or are poorly organized, and they help find ways to improve them. *Social ecologists* learn how the environment affects where and how people live. These are just a few of the many areas in which sociologists may choose to work.

Sociologists work closely with other social scientists and scientific professionals, such as statisticians, psychologists, cultural anthropologists, economists, and political scientists.

Over two-thirds of all sociologists teach in colleges and universities. They may work on sociology research projects at the same time. Other sociologists work for government agencies that deal with poverty, crime, community development, and similar social problems.

Education and Training

English, foreign languages, mathematics, sciences, and social studies classes will prepare you for a college sociology program. You need at least a bachelor's

EXPLORING

• Working on your school newspaper, magazine, or yearbook can help you to develop important interview, research, and writing skills, as well as make you more aware of your community.

• The International Sociological Association conducted an opinion survey of its members to find the most important books about sociology published in the 20th century. Here are the top five:

Economy and Society by Max Weber

The Sociological Imagination by Charles Wright Mills

Social Theory and Social Structure by Robert K. Merton

The Protestant Ethic and the Spirit of Capitalism by Max Weber

The Social Construction of Reality by P. L. Berger and T. Luckmann

ment agencies. More than half of all working sociologists have doctoral degrees. Most of them teach in colleges and universities while doing their research.

Sociologists who wish to work for the federal government may be required to take a civil service examination. Those who want to work overseas may have to take a foreign-language proficiency test. Some clinical sociologists have to be certified by the Clinical Sociology Association. This requires a doctoral degree, one year's experience as a clinical sociologist, and other proof of knowledge and skills.

degree to become a sociologist. With this education, you may be able to find a job doing interviews or collecting data. With a teaching certificate, you can teach sociology in a high school. With a master's degree, you can find jobs with research institutes, industries, or govern-

Earnings

Sociologists working as full professors in colleges and universities have average salaries of $69,924 a year at public universities, and $84,970 a year at private ones, according to a 1998 survey by the *Chronicle of Higher Education.* Associate professors at public universities made an annual average of $50,186 and $56,517 at private universities. The U.S. Department of Labor reports that median annual earnings for social scientists in 1998 were $38,990. Salaries ranged from less than $21,530 to more than $80,640.

Outlook

Overall employment of social scientists is expected to grow about as fast as the average through 2008, according to the U.S. Department of Labor. Opportunities are best for those with a doctorate and experience in fields such as demography, criminology, environmental sociology, and gerontology. Competition will be strong in all areas, as more sociology graduates continue to enter the job market than there are positions to fill.

FOR MORE INFO

For more information, contact the following organizations:

American Sociological Association
1307 New York Avenue, NW, Suite 700
Washington, DC 20005
202-383-9005
http://www.asanet.org

Society for Applied Sociology
Baylor University
PO Box 97131
Waco, TX 76798-7131
254-710-3811
http://www.appliedsoc.org

Sociologists will also find more opportunities in marketing, as companies conduct research on specific populations. The Internet is opening new areas of sociological research; sociologists, demographers, and market researchers are studying online communities and their impact on society.

Tour Guides

What Tour Guides Do

Tour guides show visitors around different museums, neighborhoods, cities, and countries. Some tour guides act as *travel agents* for the tour, booking airline flights, car rentals, and cruises. They research area hotels and other lodgings and plan sightseeing tours. Guides try to meet the needs of the group by learning individual interests. If older members of a tour, for example, cannot climb 50 steps to visit a cathedral, the tour guide plans other activities for them.

Tour guides know all about the areas they visit. A tour guide on a city tour, for example, knows that city's geography, history, art, architecture, politics, and people. Tour guides for museums know every piece in the museum's collection and can explain it clearly to tourists. They are prepared to answer all kinds of questions.

Tour guides arrange many details of each tour ahead of time, such as hotel reservations, special exhibits, theater tickets, and side trips. There are always problems that arise during trips, though, and guides must be able to handle them quickly and calmly.

Guides make sure that food and lodging meet expected standards and that all baggage and personal belongings are loaded on the plane, bus, or train. It is most important that tour guides keep track of the people on their tours. They must see that everyone returns home safely.

Education and Training

You do not need to earn a college degree to be a tour guide, but it would be helpful, especially if you hope to lead tours in foreign countries. Courses in history, geography, art, architecture, foreign languages, speech, and communication are good preparation.

Some large cities have professional schools that offer classes in guiding tours. This training may take nine to 12 months. Some community colleges offer similar training programs that last six to eight weeks. Tour guide training can include classes in geography, psychology, human relations, and communications.

EXPLORING

• Take tours of museums and other special attractions in your area. By listening and observing, you can learn about the work of a tour guide.

• Join a public speaking or debate club to work on your communication skills.

• Prepare speeches for class or community groups on local history, architecture, wildlife, or other topics of local interest. Once you have done the research for your speech, you might offer to give a tour to friends or relatives visiting from out of town.

Travel agencies and tour companies often provide their own training, which prepares guides to lead the tours their companies offer. The National Tour Association offers certification to guides who complete certain education and experience requirements.

Earnings

Tour guides usually have busy and slow periods of the year that correspond to vacation and travel seasons. Earnings range from $9.75 to $20 an hour. The average salary for an entry-level tour guide is $20,000 a year. Average mid-level earnings are about $35,000 a year. Experienced guides with managerial responsibilities can earn up to $65,000 a year. The most experienced guides can earn as much as $75,000 annually.

TRAVELERS LIKE HISTORY AND CULTURE

The Travel Industry Association of America says that cultural and historic tourism is popular. According to their survey, 53.6 million adults said they visited a museum or historical site in the past year. About 33 million American adults attended a cultural event such as a theater, arts, or music festival. The survey also showed that cultural and historic travelers:

- Spend more money

- Stay in hotels more often

- Visit more destinations

- Are twice as likely to travel for entertainment purposes than other travelers

Outlook

Because of the many different travel opportunities for business, recreation, and education, there will be a continuing need for tour guides through 2008. This demand is due in part to the strong economy, when people earn more money and are able to spend more on travel.

Tours for special interests, such as to conservation areas and wilderness destinations, continue to be popular. Another area of tourism that is growing is inbound tourism. Many foreign travelers visit U.S. tourist spots, such as Hollywood, Disney World, and Yellowstone National Park.

RELATED JOBS

Historians
Inbound Tour Guides
Museum Teachers
Travel Agents

FOR MORE INFO

For general information on the career of tour guide, contact:
National Tourism Foundation
546 East Main Street
PO Box 3071
Lexington, KY 40596-3071
800-682-8886
http://www.ntaonline.com

For information regarding its certification program and other general information concerning a career as a tour guide, contact:
The Professional Guides Association of America
2416 South Eads Street
Arlington, VA 22202-2532
703-892-5757

For information on the travel industry and the related career of travel agent, contact the following organization:
American Society of Travel Agents
1101 King Street, Suite 200
Alexandria, VA 22314
703-739-2782
http://www.astanet.com

For information on the travel industry, contact:
The Travel Industry Association of America
1100 New York Avenue, NW, Suite 450
Washington, DC 20005-3934
202-408-8422
http://www.tia.org

Glossary

accredited: Approved as meeting established standards for providing good training and education. This approval is usually given by an independent organization of professionals to a school or a program in a school. Compare **certified** and **licensed**.

apprentice: A person who is learning a trade by working under the supervision of a skilled worker. Apprentices often receive classroom instruction in addition to their supervised practical experience.

apprenticeship: 1. A program for training apprentices (see apprentice). 2. The period of time when a person is an apprentice. In highly skilled trades, apprenticeships may last three or four years.

associate's degree: An academic rank or title granted by a community or junior college or similar institution to graduates of a two-year program of education beyond high school.

bachelor's degree: An academic rank or title given to a person who has completed a four-year program of study at a college or university. Also called an undergraduate degree or baccalaureate.

certified: Approved as meeting established requirements for skill, knowledge, and experience in a particular field. People are certified by the organization of professionals in their field. Compare **accredited** and **licensed**.

community college: A public two-year college, attended by students who do not live at the college. Graduates of a community college receive an associate degree and may transfer to a four-year college or university to complete a bachelor's degree. Compare **junior college** and **technical college**.

diploma: A certificate or document given by a school to show that a person has completed a course or has graduated from the school.

doctorate: An academic rank or title (the highest) granted by a graduate school to a person who has completed a two- to three-year program after having received a master's degree.

fringe benefit: A payment or benefit to an employee in addition to regular wages or salary. Examples of fringe benefits include a pension, a paid vacation, and health or life insurance.

graduate school: A school that people may attend after they have received their bachelor's degree. People who complete an educational program at a graduate school earn a master's degree or a doctorate.

intern: An advanced student (usually one with at least some college training) in a professional field who is employed in a job that is intended to provide supervised practical experience for the student.

internship: 1. The position or job of an intern (see intern). 2. The period of time when a person is an intern.

junior college: A two-year college that offers courses like those in the first half of a four-year college program. Graduates of a junior college usually receive an associate degree and may transfer to a four-year college or university

to complete a bachelor's degree. Compare **community college.**

liberal arts: The subjects covered by college courses that develop broad general knowledge rather than specific occupational skills. The liberal arts are often considered to include philosophy, literature and the arts, history, language, and some courses in the social sciences and natural sciences.

licensed: Having formal permission from the proper authority to carry out an activity that would be illegal without that permission. For example, a person may be licensed to practice medicine or to drive a car. Compare **certified**.

major: (in college) The academic field in which a student specializes and receives a degree.

master's degree: An academic rank or title granted by a graduate school to a person who has completed a one- or two-year program after having received a bachelor's degree.

pension: An amount of money paid regularly by an employer to a former employee after he or she retires from working.

private: 1. Not owned or controlled by the government (such as private industry or a private employment agency). 2. Intended only for a particular person or group; not open to all (such as a private road or a private club).

public: 1. Provided or operated by the government (such as a public library). 2. Open and available to everyone (such as a public meeting).

regulatory: Having to do with the rules and laws for carrying out an activity. A regulatory agency, for example, is a government organization that sets up required procedures for how certain things should be done.

scholarship: A gift of money to a student to help the student pay for further education.

social studies: Courses of study (such as civics, geography, and history) that deal with how human societies work.

starting salary: Salary paid to a newly hired employee. The starting salary is usually a smaller amount than is paid to a more experienced worker.

technical college: A private or public college offering two- or four-year programs in technical subjects. Technical colleges offer courses in both general and technical subjects and award associate degrees and bachelor's degrees.

technician: A worker with specialized practical training in a mechanical or scientific subject who works under the supervision of scientists, engineers, or other professionals. Technicians typically receive two years of college-level education after high school.

technologist: A worker in a mechanical or scientific field with more training than a technician. Technologists typically must have between two and four years of college-level education after high school.

undergraduate: A student at a college or university who has not yet received a degree.

undergraduate degree: See **bachelor's degree**.

union: An organization whose members are workers in a particular industry or company. The union works to gain better wages, benefits, and working conditions for its members. Also called a labor union or trade union.

vocational school: A public or private school that offers training in one or more skills or trades. Compare **technical college**.

wage: Money that is paid in return for work done, especially money paid on the basis of the number of hours or days worked.

Index

History on the Web

A-Z History

http://school.discvery.com/homeworkhelp.worldbook/atozhistory

A New Lease on Life: Museum Conservation

http://www.cr/nps.gov/csd/exhibits/conservation/intro.htm

America's Story from America's Library

http://www.americaslibrary.gov/cgi-bin/page.cgi

The Avalon Project at the Yale Law School
Documents in Law, History, and Diplomacy

http://yale.edu/lawweb/avalon/avalon.htm

Biographical Dictionary

http://s9.com/biography

Eye Witness

http://www.ibiscom.com/

Harcourt Brace Social Studies

http://www.harcourtschool.com/menus/
harcourt_brace_social_studies.html

HyperHistory

http://www.hyperhistory.com/online_n2/History_n2/a.html